T0193925

If You Worry About Money, You Will Always Be Broke

A Pathway to A Mental, Physical, and Financial Prosperity

Teresa A. Dunbar

authorHOUSE®

AuthorHouse™
1663 Liberty Drive
Bloomington, IN 47403
www.authorhouse.com
Phone: 1 (800) 839-8640

© 2019 Teresa A. Dunbar. All rights reserved.

No part of this book may be reproduced, stored in a retrieval system, or transmitted by any means without the written permission of the author.

Published by AuthorHouse 06/19/2019

ISBN: 978-1-7283-1110-4 (sc)
ISBN: 978-1-7283-1109-8 (e)

Library of Congress Control Number: 2019942619

Print information available on the last page.

Any people depicted in stock imagery provided by Getty Images are models, and such images are being used for illustrative purposes only.
Certain stock imagery © Getty Images.

This book is printed on acid-free paper.

Because of the dynamic nature of the Internet, any web addresses or links contained in this book may have changed since publication and may no longer be valid. The views expressed in this work are solely those of the author and do not necessarily reflect the views of the publisher, and the publisher hereby disclaims any responsibility for them.

Scripture quotations marked NIV are taken from the Holy Bible, New International Version®. NIV®. Copyright © 1973, 1978, 1984 by International Bible Society. Used by permission of Zondervan. All rights reserved. [Biblica]

Scriptures marked as "(CEV)" are taken from the Contemporary English Version Copyright © 1995 by American Bible Society. Used by permission.

Scripture taken from The Voice™. Copyright © 2008 by Ecclesia Bible Society. Used by permission. All rights reserved.

Contents

Acknowlegements

Thank you, Denise Dunbar, for listening to me go on and on about the subject of this book and for taking to heart the principles of which I talk about in this book.

Thank you, Denise Smith for always being there whenever I needed to talk. You have this talent for pointing me in the right direction, showing me the light and asking me what I see. Thank you for your wisdom and guidance.

Special Thanks

Lori-Ann Wojcik
Malisa (Dunbar) Seuell
Fidel C. Jackson
Lauren Morales

Limmie Dunbar (my grandmother)
I love you and I miss you.

In loving memory of Uncle Bill

5   Trust in the LORD with all your heart
    and lean not on your own understating;
6   In all your ways submit to him,
    and he will make your paths straight.

Proverbs 3: 5-6

As you read this book, I hope you keep these essentials points in mind.

- The way you think is everything.
- Your attitude determines your altitude.
- Always be kind to others. You'll never know who you'll meet or who you'll need.
- If you worry about money, you will always to be broke.

And always remember – GOD's got your back.

*If You Worry About Money, You
Will Always Be Broke*

Worry

wor·ry | \ 'wər-ē, 'wə-rē\
verb

Mental distress or agitation resulting from concern usually for something impending or anticipated : anxiety

- ❖ to touch or disturb something repeatedly
- ❖ to assail with rough or aggressive attack or treatment : torment
- ❖ to subject to persistent or nagging attention or effort
- ❖ to afflict with mental distress or agitation: make anxious
- ❖ to move, proceed, or progress by unceasing or difficult effort : struggle
- ❖ to feel or experience concern or anxiety
- ❖ an instance or occurrence of such distress or agitation

Introduction

This book was inspired by my own life experiences. A visit from my uncle and the words he spoke inspired me to rethink the way I lived my life. I wrote this book in hopes to show others that a better way of thinking is not only possible but beneficial to our well-being. How we think is everything. If we think we can, we can, and we will. If we think we cannot, we will not.

I've learned that my destiny is in GOD's hands and that I needed to let go and let GOD. Once I stopped trying to control everything, GOD took the wheel and HE lead me where I needed to go. Don't dwell on the things you cannot control. Make the choice to change your life. Make the choice to remove negativity and doubt. Let GOD take the wheel. He knows where you need to be.

"With every experience, you alone are painting your own canvas, thought by thought, choice by choice." - **Oprah Winfrey**

"I know for sure that what we dwell on is who we become. " – **Oprah Windrey**

I wish you all the best. I am confident that what I've learned from my uncle's words of wisdom will help each of you see things in a different light. A brighter future can be yours.

Inspirational Quotes

Here is a collection of inspirational sayings that
I hope will inspire you throughout your day.

*"Have the ability to dream and the courage
to go after it."* – **Anonymous**

*"Every day is a new opportunity. You can build on
yesterday's success or put its failures behind and start
over again. That's the way life is, with a new game every
day, and that's the way baseball is."* – **Bob Feller**

*"You must be the change you wish to see in the
world."* – **Mohandas Karamchand Gandhi**

*"I am always doing that which I cannot do, in order
that I may learn how to do it."* – **Pablo Picasso**

*"What counts is not necessarily the size of the
dog in the fight – it's the size of the fight in
the dog."* – **Dwight D. Eisenhower**

*"Twenty years from now you will be more disappointed
by the things that you didn't do then by the ones you did*

do. So throw off the bowlines. Sail away from the safe harbor. Catch the trade winds in your sails. Explore. Dream. Discover." – **H. Jackson Brown, Jr.**

"It's not whether you get knocked down, it's whether you get up." – **Vince Lombardi**

"A journey of a thousand leagues begins beneath one's feet". – **Lao Tzu**

"What lies behind us and what lies before us are tiny matters compared to what lies within us". – **Henry s. Haskins**

"Challenge yourself with something you know you could never do, and what you'll find is that you can overcome anything." – **Anonymous**

"All our dreams can come true, if we have the courage to pursue them". – **Walt Disney**

"I've missed more than 9,000 shots in my career. I've lost almost 300 games. Twenty-six times, I've been trusted to take the game-winning shot and missed. I've failed over and over and over again in my life. And that is why I succeed." – **Michael Jordan**

"I know for sure that what we dwell on is who we become." – **Oprah Windrey**

"If not us, who? If not now, when?" – **Hillel The Elder**

"The pessimist sees difficulty in every opportunity. The optimist sees the opportunity in every difficulty." –**Winston Churchill**

"The elevator to success is out of order. You'll have to use the stairs... one step at a time." – **Joe Girard**

"If you want to test your memory, try to recall what you were worrying about one year ago today." – **E. Joseph Cossman**

"What you do speaks so loudly that I cannot hear what you say". – **Ralph Waldo Emerson**

"Whether you think you can or think you can't, you're right."– **Henry Ford**

"The only thing worse than being blind is having sight but not vision." – **Helen Keller**

"The reason I've been able to be so financially successful is that my focus has never, ever for one minute been money." - **Oprah Winfrey**

"With every experience, you alone are painting your own canvas, thought by thought, choice by choice." - **Oprah Winfrey**

"I believe that one of life's greatest risks is never daring to risk." - **Oprah Winfrey**

"Don't go through life, grow through life."– **Eric Butterworth**

"If you want to make your dreams come true, the first thing you have to do is wake up"– **J. M. Power**

"Don't cry because it's over, smile because it happened."– **Theodor Seuss Geisel (Dr. Seuss)**

"Man is free at the instant he wants to be."- **Voltaire**

"There are two primary choices in life: to accept conditions as they exist or accept the responsibility for changing them."– **Denis Waitley**

"If you want to make good use of your time, you've got to know what's most important and then give it all you've got." - **Lee Iacocca**

"If you limit your choice only to what seems possible or reasonable, you disconnect yourself from what you truly want, and all that is left is a compromise." - **Robert Fritz**

"You need to forget yesterday, because it has already forgotten you. You need to stop sweating tomorrow, because you haven't even met yet. Instead you need to open your eyes and your heart to a truly precious gift; today." – **www.richdadadvisors.com**

"Don't run from tests and hardships brothers and sisters. As difficult as they are, you ultimately find joy in them; if you embrace them, your faith will blossom under pressure as you endure. And true patience brought on by endurance will equip you to complete the long journey and cross the finish line – mature, complete, and wanting nothing." – **James 1:2-4**

"Bad things do happen; how I respond to them defines my character and the quality of my life. I can choose to sit in perpetual sadness, immobilized by the gravity of my loss, or I can choose to rise from the pain and treasure the most precious gift I have - life itself." — **Walter Anderson**

Chapter One

Turn all Your Worries over to HIM

*God cares for you, so turn all your
worries over to him.* - **1 Peter 5:7**

Chapter One

Turn all your worries over to HIM

If there is ever one lesson you should learn in life, this should be one of them. If you worry about money, you will always be broke was the lesson I learned long ago. How did I stop worrying about money? I *turned all my worries over to HIM*. Before turning over my worries, I spent years worrying and wondering why I wasn't in a better place in my mind and in my life. I was stagnant mentally, physically, emotionally, financially and spiritually. What was I doing wrong? I thought I had everything under control. But one day, it all came to light.

Who is HIM? GOD. The higher power you believe in or whatever gets you through the day. Why should you turn your worries over to HIM? Because worrying is a gateway to nowhere. Life can be difficult enough without having to worry about money. Of course, we need money for food, shelter and clothing. We need money to enjoy the good things in life. If you worry about money, you will always be broke. I can attest to this because I have lived it. Sitting around worrying about money never changed or improved my situation. And it will not improve yours.

Worrying about money does not improve your health or your mental status. It does not make you stronger or wiser. Wasting time worrying is not going to get you to your destination nor is it going to make you happy. When we worry, we spend too much time in negativity, uncertainty and despair. Worrying causes depression, sadness and regret. We get stuck in a rut and we wonder how we're ever going to get out. When we waste time worrying, we are not living the life GOD intended for us. There is no joy because sadness has taken over. We start to regret the choices we've made in life. All the things we have not accomplished in life become the focus and we forget about the things we have accomplished. We become pessimistic, doubtful, and critical of ourselves.

Not only does worrying have an unpleasant outcome on our lives, it also has a negative impact on our family and friends. Worrying can cause stress and stress can impact you both mentally and physically. Stress has a significant and negative effect on your body, mind, relationships, happiness, work, and your overall health and well-being. Worrying is like a silent killer. There are no obvious symptoms and it could progress to an advance stage before we know it. Worrying about things that should be turned over to GOD destroys us from the inside out. It takes away our happiness. Worry is a powerful thing. Let's not give it that power. Let's take away worry's power and give it to GOD.

Of course, it's hard not to worry about some things. You have bills due and children to feed, tuition to pay, etc. You wonder how you're ever going to make it. You're struggling and living paycheck to paycheck. You feel as though everything is against you. I'm here to tell you that the only thing that is against you is letting worry get in the way. Most of the things we worry about will never happen and some of the things we worry about have already happened. When you spend time worrying, you spend less time living.

Think about this statement. *Let go and let GOD.* We've heard this statement many times. Yet, we can't seem to do it. We can't let go. We can't seem to turn all our worries over to HIM. HIM being your GOD. Your higher power. HIM being what keeps you going, what makes you stronger. We struggle with letting go because we tend to think that we are in control. Yes, for the most part we can control our situation. For example, we can control things like studying to get good grades, or how fast or slow we drive or how much food we eat. We can control how we feel about a situation. We try to control every aspect of our lives. Some things we can change and some things we cannot. We must choose our battles wisely. Worrying about money is a battle we don't need to fight. It's a battle we tend not to win.

> *"Letting go helps us to live in a more peaceful state of mind and helps restore our balance. It allows others to be responsible for themselves and for us to take our hands off situations that do not belong to us. This frees us from unnecessary stress."* - **Melody Beattie**

When you can let go of the things that are holding you back, you will see a difference in your outlook on life. You will notice a difference in how you feel and how you think. You will see a difference in your spiritual, financial, physical, and emotional well-being. Let go of doubt. Release worry and turn all your worries over to HIM.

"If you want to test your memory, try to recall what you were worrying about one year ago today." – **E. Joseph Cossman**

I was in your shoes once. I was going through life wondering and worrying about how I was going to make it. I worried about how I was going to pay my bills and how I was going to feed my son. I thought, *"I did everything right. I'm a good person. I take good care of my son. What was I doing wrong?"* I often thought why do so many other people have so much, and I had so little? I did not understand how I got myself in this situation. And I didn't know how I was going to get myself out of the rut I was in. What I didn't realize was that I was holding myself back. Not only did I spend too much time worrying about the things I had no control over, I spent too much time not realizing I had control over the way I think. I was going in circles and getting nowhere.

"When you worry, you go over the same ground endlessly and come out the same place you started. Thinking makes progress from one place to another; worry remains static." – **Harold Bridgewood Walker**

If I was going to do better and be better, I had to let go. I had to put a lid on all that worrying. I had to lose control. I had to stop trying to control the things I had no control over and learn to control the things in which I had control. I needed to control my attitude and my way of thinking. It wasn't easy. But anything that's worth having, never is. Obtaining a better physical, emotional, spiritual and financially sound me was the end goal. I was tired of going down that dark, endless road of doubt and self-destruction.

What are you going to do to change your attitude? How are you going to let go? What steps are you going to take to reduce or end the worrying? What's stopping you? I know, you'll start next week – right? When you spend wasted time worrying, next week turns into next month. Next month turns into next year and next year turns into the next ten years. My, my, my, where has the time gone? What are you going to do to change your situation? Are you going to hold on to worry or let go?

Worry is a verb. It is always in action. It controls your every move. It repeatedly disturbs your emotional well-being. It afflicts mental distress and agitation in your life. It aggressively attacks your happiness. Let's break this endless cycle and let's put worry to rest. We don't need it. We don't want it. Worry is not welcome here anymore.

"Every tomorrow has two handles. We can take hold of it with the handle of anxiety or with the handle of faith." – **Henry Ward Beecher**

Turn all your worries over to HIM. And I guarantee things will get better.

"Worry is not about the possible troubles of the future; for if they come, you are but anticipating and adding to their weight; and if they do not come, your worry is useless; and in either case, it is weak and vain, and a distrust of God's providence." – **Hugh Blair**

Chapter Two

Thinking Positive

"Man is free at the instant he wants to be." - **Voltaire**

Chapter Two

Thinking positive

In my mind, I was living in an unrealistic, unfulfilling, unproductive world. I was stagnant. I didn't know where I was headed, where I was going or where I wanted to go. I knew where I had been, and I knew I didn't want to go back there. But I was caught between negativity and doubt. They were my best friends and they controlled my very existence. Low self-esteem and lack of self-confidence were ahead of me. I was last in this race. What was there to be positive about? Don't get me wrong, I was blessed to have my health. I had a decent place to lay my head. I had a job and car. My son was fed. But I was broke, in debt and struggling. I couldn't get ahead. At best, I was just getting by. I knew there had to be more. But what? I didn't see the light. The tunnel was long and dark. I couldn't see in front of me. I felt a brighter future was out there, but I just couldn't reach it. Was I doomed to just getting by? My inability to see beyond my current situation was hindering me from being physically, emotionally, spiritually and financially free of the prison in which I placed myself.

> *"People become attached to their burdens sometimes more than the burdens are attached to them."* – **George Bernard Shaw**

All that I had come to know changed the day I decided to live by what I call my mantra, ***"If you worry about money, you will always be broke"***. That was the day I decided that I was not going to be a slave to negative thinking. That was the day I decided to kick negativity and doubt to the curb. I fired low self-esteem and lack of self-confidence. It was time to have a more positive attitude.

Keeping a positive attitude can be difficult at best because there is always something that can steer you away or hinder you from keeping your head up. I know. I've been there. What my uncle passed on to me, (what I didn't know at the time would define my very existence), changed my whole outlook on life. Since hearing those words, ***"If you worry about money, you will always be broke"***, I continue to work on keeping worry out of my vocabulary and maintaining a positive attitude every day. My mind is open, my attitude is positive, and my future is bright.

> *"Positive thinking is a mental and emotional attitude that focuses on the bright side of life and expects positive results. A positive person anticipates happiness, health and success, and believes he or she can overcome any obstacle and difficulty."* – **Google definition**

Thinking positively can improve your self-confidence and self-esteem tremendously. Thinking positively scares away doubt, fear and despair. It removes all shadows and provides an abundance of light. It allows you to think more clearly about your situation. You become more level headed. You won't make decisions based on fear or doubt. Thinking positively improves your demeanor. You stand straighter and taller. You feel good about yourself. Your smile is wider. You even dress better. The better you feel about yourself, the more confident you are about your life. When you have self-esteem and self-confidence, your mind is reconditioned to allow for the restructuring of your thoughts. I'm not saying that I got this self-confidence and self-esteem thing down. I work on it every day. And it's getting better day by day. It won't happen overnight, but it will happen. Just like anything else you want to accomplish, you must work at it. Just trust in yourself, keep your head up and always, I mean always, believe in yourself and have a positive attitude no matter the situation.

Be careful and take heed on how you project your image to others. Because if you don't feel it, neither will they. If you feel low and you sense negative thoughts running through your mind, don't ignore it. Explore it. You can get through this by conquering those feelings and identifying what and how you feel. If self-doubt and low self-esteem creep into your mind when you are alone, call a friend. We all have that one friend that can lift our spirits and put us back on the track to positive thinking. Always try to surround yourself with positive people.

"Surround yourself with the dreamers and the doers, the believers and thinkers, but most of all, surround yourself with those who see the greatness within you, even when you don't see it yourself." — **Edmund Lee**

If reading books on improving your self-image and thinking positive is your thing, read them. You just might learn something you didn't know about yourself. Learn new things. Boost your knowledge on what you are passionate about. You'll be able to talk proudly on the subject when you need to. The more you know, the more you grow and the more positive your attitude will become.

Take some time to get to know you. Look in the mirror, often. What do you see? Do you like what you see? Do you see someone who is intelligent, strong, and confident? Do you see someone with a bright future? Do you see someone with a positive attitude? At first, you may not. But keep looking, you will. Improvements will come in small steps. Relax. Acknowledge the small steps. No matter how small, every positive step to a better you is a step in the right direction.

There are many ways to get and keep positive energy. Meditation can be very beneficial to your overall well-being. It only takes a few minutes of your day to get in tuned with you. You can spend time pondering the meaning of life or you can spend a few moments a day in silence reducing stress and anxiety. Meditation allows you to get connected with yourself and it allows you to become more aware of who you are! And when you know who you are, you are confident in your choices. Another way I work at having a positive attitude is listening to various ministries and reading spiritual books. Read motivational books to lift your spirit. Practice thinking and writing positive statements every day.

Practice speaking positively about yourself and your surroundings every day. No one can improve you but you. No one can change your attitude, your altitude or your fortitude but you. It takes courage and sacrifice to want to do better and have a better attitude. Learning to think positive can restore and renew you.

> *"Positive thinking, transformed into positive beliefs, can be powerful in shaping our life, mind, heart and character."* - **http://www.heartfulnessmagazine.com/ power-belief-positive-thinking/**

It takes courage to want to change your life. You've been thinking negatively so long that it's going to take nerve and a fight to change what has consumed your very existence. You are going to stand up to a challenge which can be very daunting. You'll need to develop thick skin because people will look at you differently and you are going to gain a few haters. It takes courage to grow beyond the limits you have placed on yourself.

It will take some sacrifice to improve your well-being. We all know negative people and we may have a friend or two in that category. But guess what? You may have to sever your friendship with those 'negative Nancys'. You'll no longer want to be around all that negativity. There is a different path that awaits you. You'll have no time for negative people and negative thoughts.

> *"Whatever you believe in your heart to be true is a reality in your life. As a result, you then attract events, experiences and people in your life to match your 'loves' or 'beliefs'."* - **http://www.heartfulnessmagazine.com/ power-belief-positive-thinking/**

Negative thoughts narrow your mind. They hinder you

from having vision and seeing the big picture. Negative thoughts limit your options and introduce doubt. Negative thoughts can make you unhealthy and unhappy which tend to introduce fear, anger and stress. Let's get rid of bad thoughts and the stress that comes along with it. Let's beef up optimism and put pessimism out to pasture. Let's anticipate happiness, health and success. Believe you can overcome any obstacle and any difficulty that stand in your way. Let's practice the power of positive thinking.

> *"The first step toward success is taken when you refuse to be a captive of the environment in which you first find yourself."* – **Mark Caine**

Practice being grateful. There is an exercise at the end of this book that I feel will help you grow your mind, build happiness and provide positive experiences in your life. This exercise could help you feel better about yourself and your situation.

"There is a basic law that like attracts like. Negative thinking definitely attracts negative results. Conversely, if a person habitually thinks optimistically and hopefully, his positive thinking sets in motion creative forces, and success instead of eluding him flows toward him." – **Norman Vincent Peale**

Chapter Three

My Story

"A Journey of a thousand leagues begins beneath one's feet." – **Lao Tzu**

Chapter Three

My Story

From time to time it is essential that we look at where we are in our lives. Do you ever wonder, 'how did I get to this (physical and mental) place? Is this where I want to be in life? Is this where I should be in life? Am I financially where I want to be? Do I have everything I need and want?' Throughout my life I have spent more time thinking (than I care to admit), about these very things. And I thought I understood all the old clichés like, *Life is what you make it. When one door closes, another one opens and how you think is everything.* But I didn't get it. A true understanding in the form of an eye opener (a mental slap upside the head) came to me unexpectedly and my life was forever changed. A new journey began.

> *"It isn't what you have or who you are or where you are or what you are doing that makes you happy or unhappy. It is what you think about it."* - **Dale Carnegie**

Like so many of us out there, I was in debt. I had good

credit, but I had too many credit cards. I spent money that I didn't have. I lived paycheck to paycheck and I really didn't see a way out. There were two of us that I had to take care of; my son and I. Although I could provide for my son (barely), it wasn't enough. Life was hard and I felt empty inside. I was a young, single parent struggling to make ends meet. I wasn't where I should be in life and I didn't know how I was going to get there. I didn't have the things I thought I needed or wanted. The plan I had was not working.

Although I was able to pay my bills, I was still struggling. Sometimes when I cried at night, I would ask God, "What did I do wrong? What do I need to do to improve my life? How can I get out of this situation?" I wasn't where I wanted or needed to be mentally, physically, emotionally, spiritually or even financially. My son was my number one priority. He trusted me to take care of him. It was my sworn, unwritten duty to do so. But how was I going to make it when I had so little? I needed my son to see me in a positive light. So how did I end up worrying about my future and his?

I worried a lot and I was unhappy. I tried very hard to hide the unhappiness and worry on my face. I did not want my son to be subjected to my anguish and anxiety. My worries, pain and sadness were not his burden to bear. I thought that I had no one to trust in and no one to turn to. I didn't realize that all I needed to do was let go and let GOD. As with many of us growing up in the 70's, I was raised in the church. But where was GOD when I needed Him the most? How could HE leave me in this situation? Why did HE not make things right? Did HE not hear my cries? What was I doing wrong? I didn't understand that there was a better way of thinking awaiting me. I didn't understand that all I need to do was change my way of thinking.

Change my way of thinking. Who knew? I didn't know how true of a statement that was until one day my uncle came to visit. He could tell something was wrong with me because it was written all over my face. It was in my demeanor. Doubt and worry consumed me. When my uncle asked me what was wrong, I said, 'I'm broke. I have no money. I work but I'm getting nowhere'. I just knew from the words I spoke and from the sad look on my face that he would reach into his pocket and give me some money. I thought he would help me out. All I needed was a little extra to help me get by. But he didn't give me a dime. What he gave me was something profound. I didn't see it coming. He said, *"Teresa, if you worry about money, you will always be broke"*. Whaaaaat? What was I supposed to do with that? He didn't give me any money. How could this be? He knew I needed it. He knew I needed his help. We're family and families are supposed to help each other. Instead, he hugged me and went about his way. As I stood there with my mouth opened, I thought, 'I can't buy groceries with that or pay a bill. Did he not understand my dilemma? Did he not care?' But little did I know, he was helping me. He was helping me by redirecting my thinking. Instead of giving me the fish, I was forced to learn how to fish. Did GOD send him there to redirect my steps? I thought I had control of my destiny. Little did I know I was headed in a new direction.

That night I went to bed wondering if there was something in what he said. I didn't change my thinking right away and for the next several weeks, I still wondered, how could he not help me? As I began to realize that nothing in my world was changing, I had to do something to change my outlook and to improve my situation. As I thought about his words, ***"If you worry about money, you will always be broke"***, I decided that I would to the best of my ability, adhere to those words. It was hard at first, but I was determined. Things were going to get better for me. They had to. After all, what did I have to lose? I'd been down so long, the only place I could go was up. I know it is hard to put your faith out there in the atmosphere, but we do this every day in our beliefs of a higher power. So why not?

> *"There are two primary choices in life: to accept conditions as they exist, or accept the responsibility for changing them."* - **Denis Waitley**

I tried it. I couldn't believe it. It worked. My life started to get better. On my job, a manager approached me about moving into another position. I began to make more money. There was something to this not worrying thing. How did I ever get through life before? Who knew that something so simple yet so profound could change someone's total perspective on life? *"If you worry about money, you will always be broke.* These ten words would become the foundation of how I live my life today. Those ten words changed my way of thinking and they changed my life.

I learned all I know about not worrying back in the late 80's, early 90's. I was worry free and going strong until 2008, the year of the economic downturn. After I lost my job, I was unemployed for two years. Thank goodness I had a husband at the time to back me up. During the first year, even though I was looking for job, I had no worries.

I kept the faith. Bills were still getting paid. I couldn't do everything I wanted to do but for the most part, I was happy. The second year I started to wonder. Why can't I get a job? I have a degree. I have education. I have a good work history and good work ethics. Why was I not getting job offers? I'm qualified. The first year was ok because I felt like I needed a break. As I entered the second year of unemployment, my money was running thin. I started losing all I had learned. Fear, doubt and worry had made their way back into my life. I started back down the path of low self-esteem and low self-confidence. I spent many nights crying and asking GOD, why? Then one day I looked in the mirror and said to myself, Teresa, you forgot. You forgot those ten little words. Don't you remember what your uncle said you? "*If you worry about money, you will always be broke.*" Don't you remember how you lived your life after hearing those words? That year was a period I call my 'slip and fall' moment. I fell from grace. I fell from all the hard work I had put into myself. But I got back up and I once again decided to turn all my worries over to GOD. I decided not to worry about money. Within a few weeks I got a job and I've had one ever since.

Today, I am living with that same philosophy. I'm in a place where I don't need anything, and I have most everything I want. If I don't have the money for it, I don't need it. Guess what? It's true, I really don't need it. I am practically debt free. And I have a good job. I attribute this to those very words my uncle imparted onto me. (GOD rest his soul). I'll forever be grateful for his visit. I may not remember the date he came to visit, but I darn sure remember his words. So, in turn, I communicate this same knowledge to my family and friends in hope that they too can find solace in their lives as I have done.

It is with great pleasure and enthusiasm that I share this information with everyone who wants to make a change in their lives. Because not worrying about money works. I'm proud to say that I am a living witness. I hope that everyone that reads this book will find consolation in their lives and experience the joys of how not worrying about money can improve your mental, emotional, physical, spiritual and financial well-being.

'Infuse your life with action. Don't wait for it to happen. Make it happen. Make your own future. Make your own hope. Make your own love. And whatever your beliefs, honor your creator, not by passively waiting for grace to come down from upon high, but by doing what you can to make grace happen… yourself, right now, right down here on earth.' – **Bradley Whitford**

Chapter Four

Money in the Bottom of My Purse

"Empty pockets never held anyone back. Only empty heads and empty hearts can do that." - **Norman Vincent Peale**

Chapter Four

Money in the Bottom of My Purse

What do you believe in? I believe as long as I have money in the bottom of my purse I'm never broke. It's been a habit I picked up throughout the years. I don't allow myself to spend it no matter the given situation. Having money, I'm not talking about a lot, in my wallet and in my purse helped me get through the difficult times. It's kind of like my safety net; as long as it is there, I'm never broke.

I am a firm believer that if I have that money, no matter how much it is (in my purse), I will never be broke. And because I have adopted and adapted to this philosophy, I have not been without. I keep two-dollar bills in my wallet along with a blessed dollar a friend gave me. I also keep Sacagawea coins and presidential dollars in the bottom of my purse. When I change purses, every coin goes into any purse I carry. When I break a dollar bill, I throw that change into my purse to be later collected for my piggy bank.

Going through life, my thinking was limited. I didn't understand the power of not worrying about money. It has been within the last twenty-five years that I decided not to lean unto my own understanding. I climbed out of my head and tried something new. The way I was thinking (or wasn't) wasn't getting me anywhere mentally, physically or even financially. What my uncle said to me that one faithful day opened my eyes to a new way of thinking and to a new way of living. My uncle said, *Teresa, "if you worry about money, you will always be broke."* That statement, although it wasn't something I wanted to hear at the time, shook my very being and stirred up something inside me. Even today it still resonates my soul when I think about it or say it out loud.

I've always felt that there was a better life waiting for me. I knew I had to change my way of thinking so that I could better my financial future. Not only did my life change after hearing those words my uncle imparted unto me, it changed when I decided to always keep money in the bottom of my purse. This is money that I never spend. There were temptations but I held steadfast. And I'm glad I did.

You're probably thinking that a few bills and coins in your purse or wallet is not going to make a difference because you're still broke. So, you might as well spend it, right? This is the very thinking that I am trying to steer you away from. Having money in the bottom of your purse not only makes you feel good, it's kind of a safety net.

Maybe having money in the bottom of my purse is a psychological thing, but it works. I'm never broke. I knew that with my faith in GOD, a positive attitude and my new-found freedom of money woes, I would prosper beyond my previous, negative thinking.

I'm not rich. I still must work for a living. But I don't need anything, and I can't think of any material thing that

I must have. This is an awesome position to be in and I want you to be in this position as well. I know that once you adopt this way of thinking, you too will feel better about your financial situation.

"Wealth consists not of having great possessions, but in having few wants." – **Epictetus**

In addition to having money in the bottom of my purse, I like to save coins in different size bottles. My mother has been throwing pennies around her home for years and she still does that today. I didn't understand that growing up, but I guess that's her wallet. My friend keeps change everywhere in her home. I suppose that's her wallet. You get the picture. Do what you need to do to not feel broke.

If money is your hope for independence, you will never have it. - **Henry Ford**

I no longer worry about money. And I will always keep money in the bottom of my purse. How about you? Give it a try. You too will find that you will never be broke.

Chapter Five

What I learned about being broke

"If you want to make good use of your time, you've got to know what's most important and then give it all you've got." - **Lee Iacocca**

Chapter Five

What I learned about being broke

Going broke is not fun and it ultimately sucks. No one wants to go without. Unfortunately, it is a crucial part of being an adult and an essential part of growth and appreciation.

"Don't run from tests and hardships brothers and sisters. As difficult as they are, you ultimately find joy in them; if you embrace them, your faith will blossom under pressure as you endure. And true patience brought on by endurance will equip you to complete the long journey and cross the finish line – mature, complete, and wanting nothing." – **James 1:2-4**

I learned that when we have money, we don't appreciate it. We spend it as if we have a money tree in the backyard. If we have good credit and credit cards, we use them as if they will magically be paid. And then we get in debt and go broke. Here are some reasons why being broke will bring humility and respect of money to our lives.

1. Being broke strips you and your ego down. It makes you rethink your life, situation and attitude.

2. Being broke will make you understand what others go through. You'll empathize, and you'll help people in whatever way you can.

3. Being broke makes you think twice. Do you really need those shoes? You have enough handbags at home that you don't even use. You'll use that new coffee maker you got for Christmas instead of buying coffee at the coffee shop every day. And oh, the coffee seems to taste better.

4. Being broke makes you understand what life is really about. It's not about what you have. It's about who you are.

5. Being broke will make you value what you currently have.

   You will not always be broke. Have faith. Don't worry. Be strong. This too, shall pass.

Here are some things that helped me take my mind off being broke. Maybe they can also help reduce and/or eliminate the stress and worry in your life.

1. **Work on your image:** Worrying can take a toll on you and affect your health. If you can still afford to have gym membership, go to the gym. If not, go for a walk or a run. Your mind becomes clearer to think about your next game plan. Work out in your home. Dust off those old workout tapes and set aside at least 30 minutes a day. Ever notice how good you feel when you work out?

Try a new hairstyle. Do you have a friend that can give you a new hairdo or teach you how to wear makeup? Mix and match your wardrobe. You'll be surprised at the things that have come back into style. You'll look like you've been shopping.

2. **Find a new hobby**: Now with your new sense of style, maybe you can become a personal organizer and help some of your friends with organizing their homes. Maybe you are a wonderful cook or an awesome baker. Take some of those fantastic meals for lunch; your co-workers will be jealous. Or maybe there are some recipes you've always wanted to try. If you have kids, get them involved. It's fun and it's great to see their faces light up when they can say "I made that".

3. **Take the time to clean up your home and donate things you haven't worn in six months to charity:** It feels good to give to people. You'll have a cleaner home; more storage and a tax write off. Re-arrange your furniture. Do something with that old material and old curtains. Make new pillow cases for your sofa.

4. **Focus on old and new goals:** What goals have you wanted to focus on and complete? Get back into the habit of reading again. Make a goal to read one book a month. Choose your favorite author and read the series. Better yet, write a book.

5. **Put it on a bill:** You changed some habits and started saving some money. Take the extra cash and pay down debt and put the rest into a savings account. You won't be broke forever.

By the time you rearrange and re-adjust the things in your life, you won't have time to worry about money. You'll be too busy saving it.

As I stated before, who wants to be broke? Who wants to go without? No one. But if it happens, I believe we can approach it with a newfound attitude. We can come out of it with minimal scars and pain if we just rethink, restructure and regain our purpose in life.

"The pessimist sees difficulty in every opportunity. The optimist sees the opportunity in every difficulty." –
Winston Churchill

What opportunity will you see in your difficult moment?

Chapter Six

Stop Chasing Money

"The reason I've been able to be so financially successful is my focus has never, ever for one minute been money." - **Oprah Winfrey**

Chapter Six

Stop Chasing Money

Stop chasing Money. What do I mean by that? Let me explain. Quite often we exhaust our efforts and energy chasing something that we think is better for us. We go after the jobs that pay the most money. In some cases, that's fine if it is the job you truly want. Make sure it is the job that you truly enjoy getting up for in the morning.

If you take a job because you are worried about how you are going to pay your bills, and you don't really enjoy it, you are chasing money. You are not going after what is going to make you happy or what is going to be fulfilling in your life. You are chasing money. You are not pursuing your dreams. Everyone wants more money, but it doesn't come by chasing it. Money comes by doing what you love to do. Work on your dreams and passions and the money will come.

"Your work is going to fill a large part of your life, and the only way to be truly satisfied is to do what you believe is great work. And the only way to do great work is to love what you do. If you haven't found it yet, keep

> *looking. Don't settle. As with all matters of the heart, you'll know when you find it."* – **Steve Jobs**

I've spent a lot of my working years chasing money because I was worried. I had it in my mind that I had to make more money. Sometimes it didn't matter if I wanted that job or not; it paid more. Don't get me wrong, having more money is great, but not at the expense of your happiness. After taking job after job, I realized that I wasn't happy. Those jobs paid a little bit more, but they weren't the right jobs for me. I only took them for the money. I wasn't where I wanted or needed to be. I didn't learn that then. It took me a while, but now I know. If you must work, and most of us do, it is better to be where you want to be even if you make a little less money. When you find the job you want, learn all you can. Why? Because knowledge is a power that can move you throughout the company. This new knowledge may even help you start your own company. Have the ability to dream and work on making it a reality.

> *"There are two goddesses in your heart," he told them. "The Goddess of Wisdom and the Goddess of Wealth. Everyone thinks they need to get wealth first, and wisdom will come. So they concern themselves with chasing money. But they have it backwards. You have to give your heart to the Goddess of Wisdom, give her all your love and attention, and the Goddess of Wealth will become jealous, and follow you." Ask nothing from your running, in other words, and you'll get more than you ever imagined."* – **Christopher McDougall**

Work on your dreams and passions. The money will come.

- Stop focusing on making money and think about how to invest it for your future.
- Acquire the skills to achieve your dreams.
- Work on achieving your goals a bite at a time. There is nothing like the joy you'll feel after achieving each milestone toward your dream.
- Once you have fulfilled your dream and the money comes, be mindful of how you got it, where it came from and how you're going to keep it.
- What does success look like to you? Define your success and go for it.
- Pass along your knowledge and help others.

"When you have an experience as part of a dream you are chasing, it becomes a critical building block to the story and meaning of your life. Suddenly, every experience has its place, and you learn to love the negative experiences at the same time." – **Tim Denning**

Stop focusing on the **how** and focus on the **what**

What are you passionate about?

What are your dreams?

You've heard the saying,

Do what you love, and the money will come.

Guess what,

"If you worry about money, you'll always be broke."

"When you stop chasing the wrong things you give the right things a chance to catch you."- **Lolly Daskal**

Chapter Seven

The Best is Yet to Come

"Infuse your life with action. Don't wait for it to happen. Make it happen. Make your own future. Make your own hope. Make your own love. And whatever your beliefs, honor your creator, not by passively waiting for grace to come down from upon high, but by doing what you can to make grace happen... yourself, right now, right down here on Earth." - **Bradley Whitford**

Chapter Seven

The Best is Yet to Come

Don't worry. Don't fret. Don't sit around pondering the meaning of life. While we all want answers to that question, it will come in due time. Right now, take your situation and turn it around. Focus on how to change your way of thinking. Learn to manage your attitude and muster the fortitude so that you can change your altitude.

Remember that big issue (problem) you worried about? Tackle it like it was your favorite pie. But don't eat the whole pie in one sitting. Work on it in slices. Write down the things you need to tackle. If you are more visual, draw a picture of a pie and divide it into the number of slices that fits your situation. Tackle each slice until you've eaten (figuratively) the whole pie. Divide and conquer! By doing this, it's less painful mentally, emotionally and physically. Give yourself small rewards as you conquer your projects. You won't even notice how big the project was initially.

When I went to school for my MBA, I first looked at it as a big chunk of time taken from my life. I thought, 'good grief, two years of writing papers and attending classes before graduation. This is going to take forever.' Then I decided to divide the pie. I divided my total number of classes into thirds. One third for the "M". One third for the "B" and the last third for the "A". I felt victorious each time I completed a letter. Then before I knew it, I could put them all together. I had an MBA. One bite at a time. I didn't notice that two years had gone by. The best had come; graduation! What will be your best? What are you striving for?

As with all things, change takes time. It doesn't happen overnight, and it may not happen when you think it should. Understand this, with practice it will happen. Just as you must practice playing an instrument to become proficient and successful, you must practice making the changes that are necessary to get you to your destination.

I speak from experience. I've been there, done that. And I share this with you so that you too can see the possibilities. I am successful. I managed my attitude and found the courage to change my altitude. I no longer give into doubt and low self-esteem. I understand my needs and wants. And I no longer worry about money. My life is better than it used to be. And as long as I keep practicing, I will continue to be successful.

Success is not fame nor fortune for everyone. Yes, I know, we all want to be rich. No one wants to be poor or broke; we don't have to be. Success is living your life the way you want to.

My grandmother told me she was rich. I didn't understand that then. She didn't have a huge bank account or multiple stocks and bonds. She didn't have a big fancy house, or several cars parked in the driveway. She survived the great depression. She lived through the social injustices of the world. She saw the evolution of many technological advances. And she got to see the first black president. She had family she loved, and they loved her. She was rich!

As long as I could remember, she never needed anything. To have been through the things she'd been through, she had the best attitude anyone could ever have. She was rich, and she carried herself that way. No, not in a - I have more money than you have kind of a way. But in a - I have all I need kind of way. She managed her attitude and had the courage to change her altitude. She taught me a lot. I didn't know it then, but I know it now. She lived to be 96 years old before GOD called her home. She lived her best life.

> *"Your time is limited, so don't waste it living someone else's life. Don't be trapped by dogma—which is living with the results of other people's thinking. Don't let the noise of others' opinions drown out your own inner voice. And most important, have the courage to follow your heart and intuition."* – **Steve Jobs**

Decide what is success for you. Is it fame, fortune? Is it a big house? Is it a new car? Is it getting your son or daughter through college? Or, is it just being able to pay off your bills? Whatever it is, success is a state of mind. I learned that from my grandmother. Go ahead, put worry to rest. Find the courage to can change your attitude so you too can change your altitude. The best is yet to come.

Chapter Eight

Be Grateful

"Remember that happiness is a way of travel, not a destination" - **Roy L. Goodman**

Chapter Eight

Be Grateful

This chapter is dedicated to 30 days of "**A New You**". It may take longer to change your current habits, but it will happen. For the next 30 days write down at least five things you are grateful for and watch what happens. I did it and over 1500 days later, I'm still doing it. I heard about this years ago from Oprah Winfrey, but I didn't take advantage of it then. I suppose I was too lazy or too self-consumed in worry. I thought that I could control my situation. Now don't get me wrong, you can control and change your situation. You must know how to go about it the right way. I was doing it all wrong, I didn't know about the many blessings I was missing.

> *"How you start your day makes a huge difference. Twenty minutes of exercise first thing can help you be in a better mood all day. Repeating a few positive affirmations can help you focus on what is most important".* – **Jeff Haden**

One day a friend challenged me to write down the things for which I was grateful. She told me if I did this every day for 21 days, I would be amazed, and it would change my whole thought process. I started on this journey and on the 22nd day, an unexpected check came in the mail. I had overpaid on a bill by $422 and the company refund the overpayment to me. What a blessing! Writing down what I am grateful for has become my daily ritual. I don't write for the money; I write because I am truly grateful for everything I have.

You may not be happy with your current job. You may be looking for a better job or even for your dream job. My advice to you is write down every day how grateful you are to have a job. Go to work smiling, treat everyone kind and do the best you can at what you do. I don't know how long it will take for a better job to come along. No one knows. But I guarantee you, it will come. It did for me. Even though you don't have it yet, write that you are grateful for your new job. Put it out there in the atmosphere. Speak it into existence. It will happen! And be grateful for all you have.

I write that I am grateful for waking up each morning. I write that I am grateful for being in good health. I write that I am grateful that I am able to pay my bills. I write that I am grateful for everything I have and for everything GOD has done for me.

"I write about the power of trying, because I want to be okay with failing. I write about generosity because I battle selfishness. I write about joy because I know sorrow. I write about faith because I almost lost mine, and I know what it is to be broken and in need of redemption. I write about gratitude because I am thankful for all of it." – **Kristin Armstrong.**

I wrote this book because I'm a true believer that the way you think is the way it will be. As long as I kept worrying about what I didn't have, I never had. I was spinning my wheels and going nowhere. So, I took a chance. After all, what did I have to lose? I had everything to gain. Over 1500 days later I'm still writing about everything for which I'm grateful. And I don't plan to stop!

> *"Let others lead small lives, but not you. Let others argue over small things, but not you. Let others cry over small hurts, but not you. Let others leave their future in someone else's hands, but not you."* — **Jim Rohn**

At the end of this book, there is some homework. There are 30 blank pages, so you too can begin the journey that will change your way of thinking and maybe even your life.

Once you have completed this journey, please email me at worrynot2day@gmail.com and tell me about your experience. Have you learned anything about yourself? How did you feel about the exercise in this book? Has anything changed in your life? Are you in a better place mentality, physically, financially or spiritually?

Below are some ideas on how to get start on your journey.

- Create a vision board; It works!
- Find a mentor to guide you.
- Devise a strategy toward happiness and don't let others distract you.

Set some goals and never, ever give up.

'No matter what challenges or setbacks and disappointments you may encounter along the way, you will find true success and happiness if you have only one goal. There really is only one. And that is this: to fulfill the highest most truthful expression of yourself as a human being. You want to max out your humanity by using your energy to lift yourself up, your family and the people around you.' - **Oprah Winfrey**

Chapter Nine

What are you waiting for? Start Writing, Start believing, Start doing

"Make a pact with yourself today to not be defined by your past. Sometimes the greatest thing to come out of all your hard work isn't what you get for it, but what you become for it. Shake things up today! Be You... Be Free... Share." - **Steve Maraboli**

Chapter Nine

What are You Waiting For?

Start Writing

Day 1   Date: _____

1. _____
2. _____
3. _____
4. _____
5. _____
6. _____
7. _____
8. _____
9. _____
10. _____

Notes:

_____
_____
_____
_____
_____
_____
_____

Day 2   Date: _____

1. _____
2. _____
3. _____
4. _____
5. _____
6. _____
7. _____
8. _____
9. _____
10. _____

Notes:

_____
_____
_____
_____
_____
_____
_____
_____
_____
_____

Day 3   Date: _____

1. _____
2. _____
3. _____
4. _____
5. _____
6. _____
7. _____
8. _____
9. _____
10. _____

Notes:

_____
_____
_____
_____
_____
_____
_____
_____
_____
_____

Day 4   Date: _____

1. _____
2. _____
3. _____
4. _____
5. _____
6. _____
7. _____
8. _____
9. _____
10. _____

Notes:

_____
_____
_____
_____
_____
_____
_____
_____
_____
_____

Day 5   Date: _____

1. _____
2. _____
3. _____
4. _____
5. _____
6. _____
7. _____
8. _____
9. _____
10. _____

Notes:

_____
_____
_____
_____
_____
_____
_____
_____
_____
_____

Day 6   Date: _____

1. _____
2. _____
3. _____
4. _____
5. _____
6. _____
7. _____
8. _____
9. _____
10. _____

Notes:

_____
_____
_____
_____
_____
_____
_____
_____
_____
_____

Day 7   Date: _____

1.   _____
2.   _____
3.   _____
4.   _____
5.   _____
6.   _____
7.   _____
8.   _____
9.   _____
10. _____

Notes:

_____
_____
_____
_____
_____
_____
_____
_____
_____
_____

Day 8   Date: _____

1. _____
2. _____
3. _____
4. _____
5. _____
6. _____
7. _____
8. _____
9. _____
10. _____

Notes:

_____
_____
_____
_____
_____
_____
_____
_____
_____
_____

Day 9   Date: _____

1. _____
2. _____
3. _____
4. _____
5. _____
6. _____
7. _____
8. _____
9. _____
10. _____

Notes:

_____
_____
_____
_____
_____
_____
_____
_____
_____
_____

Day 10   Date: _____

1. _____
2. _____
3. _____
4. _____
5. _____
6. _____
7. _____
8. _____
9. _____
10. _____

Notes:

_____
_____
_____
_____
_____
_____
_____
_____
_____
_____

Day 11   Date: _____

1. _____
2. _____
3. _____
4. _____
5. _____
6. _____
7. _____
8. _____
9. _____
10. _____

Notes:

_____
_____
_____
_____
_____
_____
_____
_____
_____
_____
_____

Day 12   Date: _____

1. _____
2. _____
3. _____
4. _____
5. _____
6. _____
7. _____
8. _____
9. _____
10. _____

Notes:

_____
_____
_____
_____
_____
_____
_____
_____
_____
_____

Day 13   Date: _____

1. _____
2. _____
3. _____
4. _____
5. _____
6. _____
7. _____
8. _____
9. _____
10. _____

Notes:

_____
_____
_____
_____
_____
_____
_____
_____
_____
_____

Day 14   Date: _____

1. _____
2. _____
3. _____
4. _____
5. _____
6. _____
7. _____
8. _____
9. _____
10. _____

Notes:

_____
_____
_____
_____
_____
_____
_____
_____
_____
_____

Day 15   Date: _____

1. _____
2. _____
3. _____
4. _____
5. _____
6. _____
7. _____
8. _____
9. _____
10. _____

Notes:

_____
_____
_____
_____
_____
_____
_____
_____
_____
_____
_____

Day 16   Date: _____

1. _____
2. _____
3. _____
4. _____
5. _____
6. _____
7. _____
8. _____
9. _____
10. _____

Notes:

_____
_____
_____
_____
_____
_____
_____
_____
_____
_____

Day 17 Date: _____

1. _____
2. _____
3. _____
4. _____
5. _____
6. _____
7. _____
8. _____
9. _____
10. _____

Notes:

_____
_____
_____
_____
_____
_____
_____
_____
_____
_____

Day 18   Date: _____

1. _____
2. _____
3. _____
4. _____
5. _____
6. _____
7. _____
8. _____
9. _____
10. _____

Notes:

_____
_____
_____
_____
_____
_____
_____
_____
_____
_____
_____

Day 19   Date: _____

1. _____
2. _____
3. _____
4. _____
5. _____
6. _____
7. _____
8. _____
9. _____
10. _____

Notes:

_____
_____
_____
_____
_____
_____
_____
_____
_____
_____

Day 20   Date: _____

1. _____
2. _____
3. _____
4. _____
5. _____
6. _____
7. _____
8. _____
9. _____
10. _____

Notes:

_____

_____

_____

_____

_____

_____

_____

_____

_____

_____

Day 21   Date: _____

1. _____

2. _____

3. _____

4. _____

5. _____

6. _____

7. _____

8. _____

9. _____

10. _____

Notes:

_____

_____

_____

_____

_____

_____

_____

_____

_____

_____

Day 22   Date: _____

1. _____
2. _____
3. _____
4. _____
5. _____
6. _____
7. _____
8. _____
9. _____
10. _____

Notes:

_____

_____

_____

_____

_____

_____

_____

_____

_____

_____

Day 23   Date: _____

1. _____
2. _____
3. _____
4. _____
5. _____
6. _____
7. _____
8. _____
9. _____
10. _____

Notes:

_____
_____
_____
_____
_____
_____
_____
_____
_____
_____

Day 24   Date: _____

1. _____
2. _____
3. _____
4. _____
5. _____
6. _____
7. _____
8. _____
9. _____
10. _____

Notes:

_____

_____

_____

_____

_____

_____

_____

_____

_____

_____

Day 25   Date: _____

1. _____
2. _____
3. _____
4. _____
5. _____
6. _____
7. _____
8. _____
9. _____
10. _____

Notes:

_____
_____
_____
_____
_____
_____
_____
_____
_____
_____

Day 26   Date: _____

1. _____
2. _____
3. _____
4. _____
5. _____
6. _____
7. _____
8. _____
9. _____
10. _____

Notes:

_____
_____
_____
_____
_____
_____
_____
_____
_____
_____

Day 27   Date: _____

1. _____
2. _____
3. _____
4. _____
5. _____
6. _____
7. _____
8. _____
9. _____
10. _____

Notes:

_____
_____
_____
_____
_____
_____
_____
_____
_____
_____
_____

Day 28   Date: _____

1. _____
2. _____
3. _____
4. _____
5. _____
6. _____
7. _____
8. _____
9. _____
10. _____

Notes:

_____
_____
_____
_____
_____
_____
_____
_____
_____
_____

Day 29   Date: _____

1. _____
2. _____
3. _____
4. _____
5. _____
6. _____
7. _____
8. _____
9. _____
10. _____

Notes:

_____
_____
_____
_____
_____
_____
_____
_____
_____
_____

Day 30   Date: _____

1. _____
2. _____
3. _____
4. _____
5. _____
6. _____
7. _____
8. _____
9. _____
10. _____

Notes:

_____
_____
_____
_____
_____
_____
_____
_____
_____
_____

Chapter Ten

Questions, thoughts and comments

"Success is a state of mind. If you want success, start thinking of yourself as a success." - **Joyce Brothers**

Chapter Ten

Questions, thoughts and comments

Take a few moments to answer the questions below. Take some time to reflect upon them. Then, answer them. You'll wonder why you ever wasted time worrying in the first place.

1. How do you define success?

   _____

   _____

   _____

   _____

   _____

   _____

   _____

2. How did your grateful writing exercise make you feel?

   _____

   _____

   _____

   _____

_____

_____

_____

3. Did you learn anything about yourself? _____

_____

_____

_____

_____

_____

4. Did anything positive or negative happen?

_____

_____

_____

_____

_____

5. Has your outlook on money changed?

_____

_____

_____

_____

_____

6. Will you continue to journal?

_____

_____

_____

_____

_____

_____

_____

7. Do you find the information in this book beneficial?

_____

_____

_____

_____

_____

_____

_____

8. Other thoughts/questions/Comments:

_____

_____

_____

_____

_____

_____

_____

Conclusion

Thank you for purchasing this book. Also, please thank yourself for having the courage to want to make a change for you and your family.

I hope that you found this book beneficial and I hope that you will share these words of wisdom, *"If you worry about money, you will always be broke"*, to anyone that needs to hear them.

Research

I did a little research and found some interesting sites that I thought would be beneficial in your journey to a worry-free life.

1. Building Self-Confidence
   https://www.mindtools.com/selfconf.html

2. 63 Ways to Build Self-Confidence
   http://www.lifehack.org/articles/lifestyle/63-ways-to-build-self-confidence.html

3. 25 Killer Actions to Boost Your Self-Confidence
   http://zenhabits.net/25-killer-actions-to-boost-your-self-confidence/

4. 5 Powerful Ways to Boost Your Confidence
   http://www.inc.com/peter-economy/5-powerful-ways-to-boost-your-confidence.html

5. How to Have an Awesome Day: 7 Questions to Ask Yourself Every Morning - BY JEFF HADEN
   http://www.inc.com/jeff-haden/want-to-have-a-

great-day-7-questions-to-ask-yourself-every-morning.html?cid=readmoretext1

6. Building Confidence
http://www.skillsyouneed.com/ps/confidence.html

7. Improving Self-Esteem
http://www.skillsyouneed.com/ps/self-esteem.html

8. 30 Inspiring Quotes from Oprah Winfrey
http://parade.com/453846/jerylbrunner/30-inspiring-quotes-from-oprah-winfrey/

9. 24 Quotes on Success from Oprah Winfrey
https://www.entrepreneur.com/article/269979

10. Top 100 Money Quotes of all Time
http://www.forbes.com/sites/robertberger/2014/04/30/top-100-money-quotes-of-all-time/#436dbc56675e

11. 8 Reasons Why Being Broke Will Help You Grow as A Person
http://elitedaily.com/life/8-reasons-going-broke-great-growth/

12. "The Power of I Am" – Joel Osteen
https://www.joelosteen.com/Pages/Home.aspx

13. How Positive Thinking Builds Your Skills, Boosts Your Health, and Improves Your Work – by James Clear

http://jamesclear.com/positive-thinking

14. Brainy Quotes
    https://www.brainyquote.com/quotes/quotes/d/
    devalpatri678458.html?src=t_better_way

15. 6 Reasons to Chase Your Dream Not the Money
    by Tim Denning

    Tim is best known as a long-time contributor on
    Addicted2Success. Tim's content has been shared
    hundreds of thousands of times and he has written
    multiple viral posts all around success, personal
    development, motivation, and entrepreneurship.
    During the day Tim works with the most iconic
    tech companies in the world, as an adviser, to
    assist them in expanding into Australia. By night,
    Tim coaches his students on the principles of
    personal development and the fundamentals of
    entrepreneurship. You can connect with Tim
    through his website **www.timdenning.net** or
    through his Facebook.

    https://addicted2success.com/success-advice/6-
    reasons-to-chase-your-dream-not-the-money/

"Sometimes you have to stop worrying, wondering and doubting. Have faith that things will work out, maybe not how you planned but just how its meant to be" - **Anonymous**

A Final Word From Teresa

Thank yourself for choosing to make your life better. This is the beginning of your journey. A life long journey. It is time for you to choose happiness. It is time for you to stop worrying about the things you cannot change and change the things you can – your thinking.

Serenity Prayer
- Reinhold Niebuhr (1892 – 1971)

God grant me the serenity
to accept the things I cannot change;
couage to changes the things I can;
and the wisdom to know the difference.

If You Worry About Money, You Will Always Be Broke

Do you ever wonder why it seems like you never get anywhere financially? Do you ever wonder, 'how did I get to this (physical and mental) place? Is this where I want to be in life? Is this where I should be in life? Am I financially where I want to be? Do I have everything I need and want?

You work hard to provide for your family. As hard as you work, you're still in the same place (financially). Well, did you know that as long as you worry about money, you will always be broke?

In this book, Teresa shares her story about how some unwelcomed words of wisdom changed her whole outlook on how she viewed her financial situation. After taking to heart those ten little words her uncle imparted onto her, she understood what she needed to do to change everything she had come to know. Teresa is now happier and wiser about her financial future. And she wants you to be happier and wiser too. Take the journey. You'll be surprised.

About The Author

Teresa A. Dunbar is a naïve of Chicago and a graduate of Northwestern University. She also has an MBA from the University of Phoenix. She raised her son as a single parent living paycheck to paycheck until a visit from her uncle changed her life. His words of wisdom inspired her to wake up and see things in a different light. In this book, she is sharing that wisdom with you in hopes that you too find your way.

She a true believer that the way you think is the way it will be. She believes if you keep worrying about what you don't have, you won't have. She has been practicing what she preaches for over 30 years. She has inspired her family and friends to rethink, restructure and redesign their thinking toward a more prosperous life. She continues her journey through this mental, physical, spiritual, and financial path through life and she welcomes you to come along.

If you have found this book to be beneficial and have found that it has helped you think more positive about your life, please share your thoughts at worrynot2day@gmail.com.

Printed in the United States
By Bookmasters